RELENTLESS

Joy

A BIBLE STUDY OF PHILIPPIANS
ON HOW TO LIVE A JOYFUL LIFE

Christina Patterson

Rejoice IN THE LORD *Always*

TABLE OF *Contents*

ABOUT THE AUTHOR *Christina Patterson*

Christina Patterson is an author, Bible teacher, and speaker passion-
ate about empowering women in the love of Jesus Christ and the
truth of God's Word. Through sound biblical teaching and a true
passion for the hearts of God's daughters, Christina is compelling
women to find freedom, wholeness, and satisfaction in Jesus Christ.
Christina holds a Master's degree in Theological Studies from Liber-
ty University and is the author of several books including "Mom
Enough" and "Daughters of Fire." She is the Founder and President
of Beloved Women, Inc., a non-profit providing resources and
community for women to truly know who they are in Christ: His
Beloved. Learn more at: www.belovedwomen.org.

INTRODUCTION

As I made my way to Bible study in college one evening, I had no idea the life-changing impact that one hour would hold. I walked into the small room, found a seat, and looked up to discover we would have a new teacher. As she taught, she captivated my attention because first, she was a woman. Up until that point, I had never seen many women teach the Bible. But even more than that, I was captivated because of the conviction and passion with which she taught. Her teaching on Philippians would lead this book of the Bible to become my favorite. Her exposition on Philippians 3 ignited my heart with a passion to truly know God.

The Apostle Paul wrote this letter to the church in Philippi at a time of great uncertainty. He was in prison and not sure if he will live or die. The call on his life as an apostle of the Gospel of Jesus Christ would cost him everything; his comfort, his prestige, and now maybe even his life. However, he did not write to the Philippians to complain about his situation. He did not ask for help. He wrote to gush over how joyful he was in Christ and his hope for them to experience this same joy. For every reason Paul had to be discouraged, he relentlessly found more reasons to be joyful.

One major theme we'll see in the book of Philippians is joy. In the midst of Paul's heartfelt letter to the Philippians, we learn what practices lead to a joyful life in Christ, no matter what difficulties or uncertainties we may face. I'm so excited to share these lessons and insights with you as we study the book of Philippians to know Christ more and develop a relentless joy.

Love,

Christina

HOW TO USE THIS *Bible Study* BOOK

The "Relentless Joy" Bible Study takes you through the book of Philippians to learn how to experience a joyful life in Christ. Each session is designed to help you practically understand and apply lessons from Philippians to your everyday life. This study aligns with the "Relentless Joy" Video Bible Study series; however, this video series is not necessary to complete this study.

HOW TO STRUCTURE THIS STUDY

This study is excellent for personal or group use and was designed for you to complete at your own pace. The study consists of 12 sessions which may be completed over 12 days, 12 weeks, or even 12 months depending on how often you meet with your study group or how often you plan for personal study.

Each chapter in Philippians is covered in the following sessions:
- Philippians Chapter 1: Sessions 1-3
- Philippians Chapter 2: Sessions 4-7
- Philippians Chapter 3: Sessions 8-9
- Philippians Chapter 4: Sessions 10-12

READING

Each session starts with a reading assessment. This is the scripture that will be covered in that session. Reading this scripture will be necessary to answer your study guide questions.

KEY INSIGHT

In each session, Christina provides key insights from your reading. This section provides guided commentary on a major lesson from each session's text.

VIEWER GUIDE

If you're completing this study guide along with the 12 session "Relentless Joy" video series, your viewer guide will help you to follow along with these videos. This viewer guide provides an outline from Christina's video teaching with blanks to be filled in. The "Relentless Joy" videos are found at www.belovedwomen.org for free. To download ad-free, full length videos to watch without internet access visit www.thebelovedboutique.com. Viewer guide answers can be found at the back of this study book.

STUDY QUESTIONS

Study questions are provided for each session. These questions correspond to your assigned reading and are designed to help you think more in-depth on the major themes that arise. Study questions also assist in discovering how you may apply lessons learned to your everyday life. These questions are great for both group or personal use. Space is provided under each study question for you to write your answers.

JOURNAL PROMPT

To make your study even more personal journal prompts are provided in each session. Free space is provided for you to write about and process your personal thoughts on each session's major themes.

GOING DEEPER WITH THE LIFE BIBLE JOURNAL

The LIFE Bible Journal was created to help you intentionally engage God's Word. Using our 4 "R"s Bible Study method, each study page guides you through the scriptures helping you to simply pull out meaning from the text and apply what you've learned to your everyday life. You can learn more about this method at the back of this study guide. The "Going Deeper with the LIFE Bible Journal" section at the end of each session provides more questions that specifically coordinate with your LIFE Bible Journal. These journals may be found at www.thebelovedboutique.com.

NOTES

Notes pages are provided at the end of each session for you to write any additional thoughts you may have while completing this study.

A CLOSER LOOK

Throughout this study you will find articles to help you take a closer look at the topic of joy. These extra readings provide practical ways to better understand how to experience the joy of the Lord.

HE WHO
BEGAN A
Good Work
IN YOU WILL
BRING IT TO
Completion

PHILIPPIANS 1:6

Session 1:

HE WHO BEGAN A GOOD WORK IN YOU WILL BRING IT TO COMPLETION

READING

Philippians 1:1-11

FOCUS VERSE

> *"And I am sure of this, that he who began a good work in you will bring it to completion at the day of Jesus Christ." – Philippians 1:6 ESV*

KEY INSIGHT

In Philippians chapter one we learn that Paul is joyful because of his confidence in God to finish the good work he started with the Philippian church. Why would this bring Paul joy? Because if God is in control, then the limits placed on Paul by his imprisonment would not stop his work at the Church of Philippi. This was a work that God started, and a work that He too would complete. What freedom and joy we may experience when we realize that although the work is up to us, the results are up to God. When we realize it is the power of God that starts and ends a matter we are released of the stress, anxiety, and pressure of trying to do what only God can do. All we then need to do is be obedient and let God do His part. 1 Corinthians 3:7 confirms this truth:

> *"So neither he who plants nor he who waters is anything, but only God who gives growth."- 1 Corinthians 3:7 ESV*

We rob ourselves of joy when we don't believe God will finish what He's started in our lives. We rob ourselves of peace when we feel everything is up to us. Peace and joy belong to those who trust God will do it, no matter how it looks.

Paul could have been stressed. He could have easily been worried that all the work he put into establishing this church would have been in vain because he was away, confined, restrained, and unable to control the circumstances in his own might. But you'll find no anxiety in his words. Just joy because he knows if God established this church, surely He will sustain it.

So many times we place unnecessary demands, pressure, and obligations on ourselves. We tell ourselves what we need and have to do. We run around frantically trying to keep all the pieces of our lives together with the pressure on our shoulders to ensure everything doesn't fall apart.

This pressure does not come from God. Free yourself with this truth: Do your best, and let God do the rest. Do your part but don't forget God is faithful to do His. Paul didn't just think this was true and he didn't simply hope this was true. He was sure of it. Are you?

SESSION ONE VIEWER GUIDE

Directions: Watch Session 1 of the "Relentless Joy" Video Bible Study series and fill in the blanks below.

Joy is the unconditional positive emotional state that God gives to believers through the Holy Spirit.

3 Reasons for Paul's Joy:

1. First, Paul is joyful because of the
1._____ he shares with the Philippians in the Gospel of Jesus Christ.

2. The second reason Paul is joyful is because of his confidence in God to finish the
2._____ he started at this church with the Philippians.

> We rob ourselves of
> 3._____ when we feel everything
> is up to us.

3. The third reason for Paul's thankfulness and joy is because of the

4._____ that he and the Philippians share. God's grace does not
5._____.

Our 6._____ may limit and stop us, but by God's grace, they will not stop Him.

When we choose to be thankful, we choose to be 7._____.

Paul prays that the Philippians will grow in maturity and holiness so that God may receive 8._____ and 9._____.

We can't have the clarity of mind to know what's 10._____ when we're distracted with what's simply good.

VIDEO NOTES:

SESSION ONE STUDY QUESTIONS

1. Paul proudly introduces himself as a servant of Christ when he could have bragged about his titles and accomplishments. Why do you think it was important for Paul to introduce himself this way? How does having a servant's heart lead to more joy in our lives?

2. We learn in Galatians 5:22-23 that joy is a fruit of the Holy Spirit. How does understanding that joy is a fruit of the Spirit (a gift from God) develop your thinking on what joy is and how to experience joy in your life?

3. Thanksgiving is a key practice Paul demonstrates to experience joy. Why do you think it is easier to focus on what's going wrong in our lives and forget to be thankful for what's going well?

4. Paul is thankful for the partnership He has with the Philippians. Do you have a local body of believers you can connect with that can strengthen and encourage you? Why is this important?

5. We live in a culture filled with striving, staying busy, and the constant feeling that everything is up to us. Have you ever found yourself stressed with this thinking? Share about this time.

6. Paul comforts believers with the truth that, what God starts, He will also finish. How does this truth help you change how you look at the stresses you shared in the previous question?

7. Prayer is another key practice we see Paul demonstrate in this sessions reading. Why is prayer an important part of living a joyful life? How can you cultivate a life filled with prayer?

JOURNAL PROMPT

When you look at some of the challenges you are facing, what do you still have to be grateful for in spite of your circumstance?

_____
_____
_____
_____
_____
_____
_____
_____
_____
_____
_____
_____
_____
_____
_____
_____
_____
_____
_____

GOING _Deeper_ WITH YOUR LIFE BIBLE JOURNAL

Reading: Philippians 1:1-11
READ: Who is writing this letter and why? How is the writer encouraging the readers?
REFLECT: Why is the writer so joyful?
RESPOND: What habits can we practice as believers to cultivate more joy in our lives?
REQUEST: Pray for wisdom and power to develop habits that help you to experience more of the Lord's joy in your life.

SESSION ONE NOTES

CHRIST IS
Proclaimed
AND IN THAT I
Rejoice

PHILIPPIANS 1:18

Session 2: FIGHT FOR YOUR JOY

READING

Philippians 1:12-18

FOCUS VERSE

> "What then? Only that in every way, whether in pretense or in truth, Christ is proclaimed, and in that I rejoice. Yes, and I will rejoice." - Philippians 1:18 ESV

KEY INSIGHT

Paul is very intentional to remain positive even in his imprisonment. He is so adamant to find joy even in this situation it's like a direct assault against any discouragement or doubt that may come his way. Through the example of Paul we learn joy is a choice but sometimes it is a choice we must fight for.

The Philippians could have seen Paul's imprisonment as a defeat, failure, or a sign that their faith and Paul's work were in vain. This may be a major reason why Paul wrote this letter in the first place. He wanted to assure his Philippian brothers and sisters that his imprisonment was not a sign of defeat. Paul is painting a clear picture for the Philippians to see beyond what's happening and to help them understand how even this has happened "to advance the Gospel" (Philippians 1:12 ESV) and complete the purposes that God called him to.

This brought Paul joy because he understood that the very thing meant to hold you back, is the very thing God will use to complete His work in your life. His imprisonment was the cause of the Gospel's advancement. We see God move in this way throughout scripture.

The very flames King Nebuchadnezzar used to try to kill Shadrach, Meshach, and Abednego are the same flames that destroyed the shackles meant to hold them hostage while not harming a single hair on their heads. (Daniel 3)

The thorn in Paul's side meant to weaken him was the same thing that caused the power of God to rest on him. (2 Corinthians 12:1-10)

The crucifixion that meant to humiliate and kill Jesus was the very situation that afforded eternal life to all who would believe in Him and gave Christ all authority in heaven and earth. (Matthew 28:18)

Sometimes the opposition, failure, lack, weakness, hurt, suffering, detours, and disappointment that we face in life are not signs that we're doing something wrong, as we're commonly lead to believe. They are not signs that we need to stop or quit while we're ahead. Sometimes our suffering means we're doing life right. It's the very sign that we should keep going and keep fighting for our joy.

SESSION TWO VIEWER GUIDE

Directions: Watch Session 2 of the "Relentless Joy" Video Bible Study series and fill in the blanks below.

We experience joy when we fulfill God's
1._____ on our lives.

Paul's imprisonment caused three major things to happen:

1. The prison guards and others saw that Paul was in prison 2._____.
2. Paul's "brothers" (his fellow Christians) have become more confident and bold "to speak the word without 3._____."
(Philippians 1:14 ESV)
3. Christ is 4._____.

Joy is a choice but sometimes it is a choice we must 5._____ for.

As Christians, we should never look at another believer as 6._____.

God cares that our motivation is
7._____.

8._____ is the gift that God grants us to see his provision, faithfulness, and goodness even when it's dark.

VIDEO NOTES:

SESSION TWO STUDY QUESTIONS

1. Joy is ours to choose but sometimes that choice is a fight. What encourages you to fight for joy?

2. What situations and circumstances make fighting for joy even more difficult? How can you trust God with those difficulties as you fight?

3. Paul had joy because he realized even his imprisonment was turning out for good. How does learning that God's plan can't be stopped by our challenges encourage you to keep fighting for joy?

4. Paul tells Himself that he will rejoice. What are you telling yourself in the face of difficulties that challenge your joy? Are you telling yourself the truth about God's power or are you more focused on your challenges and trials?

5. Paul was not interested in challenging or competing with those that opposed and didn't like him. Do you ever find yourself too focused on what others think of you? Do you compare yourself to others? Why is this not helpful when it comes to finding the strength to fight for your joy?

6. Joy is a gift from God. What ways can you personally fight to ensure you experience this joy that is yours in Christ?

JOURNAL PROMPT

Take time to write the greatest challenges to your joy right now and why God is greater than each challenge.

_____

_____

_____

_____

_____

_____

_____

_____

_____

_____

_____

_____

_____

_____

_____

_____

_____

_____

_____

_____

GOING *Deeper* WITH YOUR LIFE BIBLE JOURNAL

Reading: Philippians 1: 12-18
READ: What challenges does Paul reveal he is facing?
REFLECT: Why is Paul able to face these challenges with joy?
RESPOND: What things can you do to fight for your joy when life gets hard?
REQUEST: Pray to the Lord for strength to fight for the joy that is gracefully yours in Jesus Christ.

SESSION TWO NOTES

TO LIVE IS
Christ
TO DIE IS
Gain

PHILIPPIANS 1:18

$\mathcal{S}ession$ 3: A HOPE THAT LEADS TO JOY

READING

Philippians 1:19-30

FOCUS VERSE

> *"For to me to live is Christ, and to die is gain." - Philippians 1:21 ESV*

KEY INSIGHT

When we stop living for ourselves and truly live for Christ, we find a joy that can never be taken away by people, situation, failure, lack, weakness or suffering. If people did not give us joy, then people cannot take it away.

For this reason, Paul records one of the most popular and moving scriptures of all time:

> *"For to me to live is Christ and to die is gain." – Philippians 1:21 ESV*

Many of us wonder how we too may mature to this level of thinking. Paul, being through battle after battle, and prison after prison continually saw the faithfulness of God in all circumstances. He concluded if God's faithfulness is true in life, certainly it is true in death. He was ready for both and for that reason he had a sustaining joy.

From Paul's example we learn:

Joy isn't everything being perfect in your life. Joy is knowing God is working everything out for your good and His glory.

Joy isn't bad things never happening to you. Joy is knowing that God is with you in the valley.

Joy isn't having everything you want. Joy is the satisfaction of knowing Christ is enough and God's grace is sufficient.

Joy isn't understanding how everything will work out. Joy is trusting God has everything under control.

Joy is not centered on who we are, what's happening in our lives, or what will happen. Joy is centered on the fact that God is God and He will not change.

God will always provide, He will always be with us, His purposes will be fulfilled, He will be glorified, and He is in control. Because God is who our joy rests on, joy is always ours to choose.

SESSION THREE VIEWER GUIDE

Directions: Watch Session 3 of the "Relentless Joy" Video Bible Study series and fill in the blanks below.

Paul doesn't expect things to turn out how he wants. He expects God's
1._____ to be fulfilled.

If people did not give us
2._____ then people cannot take it away.

Joy isn't having everything you
3._____. Joy is the satisfaction of knowing Christ is enough and God's grace is
4._____.

Joy is a benefit of our 5._____in God

Many times our joy is not realized because our hope is in the
6._____ place.

Three ways to live a life worthy of the Gospel:
1. Live a life 7._____ with other believers.
2. Stand firm in the 8._____.
3. Consider belief in Christ and suffering for Him as a 9._____.

The 10._____ enables us to do things in this world that are not of this world.

VIDEO NOTES:

SESSION THREE STUDY QUESTIONS

1. Although Paul faced many uncertainties, his hope and expectation in the Lord gave him confidence that despite the outcome things would work out for his deliverance. Where can you place your hope and expectation to hold this same faith in the face of uncertainty?

2. When we place our hope in God, His faithfulness acts as an anchor to our souls in times of uncertainty. Read the scriptures below and write down the promise of God each reveals for you to hold and cherish.

    1. I John 1:9 _____
    2. Matthew 28:20 _____
    3. Jeremiah 29:11 _____
    4. Matthew 11:28 _____
    5. Isaiah 40:29 _____

3. What other promises can you think of that God offers His children?

4. What promise listed in the previous questions give you the most comfort, peace, and assurance. Why?

5. In this session, we learned that if people did not give us joy then people cannot take our joy away. What can you do to ensure others don't have such free access to determine how much of God's joy you experience in your life?

6. In this session we cover one of the most popular verses in Philippians: "For to me to live is Christ, and to die is gain." - Philippians 1:21 ESV Why do you think Paul was still joyful in the face of death?

7. Many times our joy is not realized because our hope is in the wrong place. Do you ever attach your joy to results and how things turn out? Why?

8. Paul charges the Philippians to live a life worthy of the Gospel (Philippians 1:27). What does it mean and look like to you to live a life worthy of the Gospel?

JOURNAL PROMPT

Write down the hopes that are currently on your heart. How do you see God's faithfulness in these hopes even if you haven't seen results?

_____

_____

_____

_____

_____

_____

_____

_____

_____

_____

_____

_____

_____

_____

_____

_____

_____

_____

_____

_____

GOING *Deeper* WITH YOUR LIFE BIBLE JOURNAL

Reading: Philippians 1:19-30
READ: Although Paul faces many uncertainties what is he sure of?
REFLECT: Why is Paul so sure the result of his imprisonment will turn out for his deliverance?
RESPOND: How can you live a life more focused on God than results?
REQUEST: Pray for wisdom to see God in all your circumstances no matter how they turn out.

SESSION THREE NOTES

COUNT IT ALL JOY

One of the most significant challenges to our ability to experience the joy of the Lord often occurs when we face tests and trials in life. It's hard to be joyful when nothing seems to go our way. However, as believers in Christ, joy is ours no matter our situation. So how do we maintain joy in the midst of trials?

We can find the answer to this question in James 1:2-5:

"Count it all joy, my brothers, when you meet trials of various kinds, for you know that the testing of your faith produces steadfastness. And let steadfastness have its full effect, that you may be perfect and complete, lacking in nothing. If any of you lacks wisdom, let him ask God, who gives generously to all without reproach, and it will be given him." – James 1:2-5 ESV

James' letter starts with him telling his brothers and sisters in Christ to count it all joy when they face trials of various kinds. There are two things we should take from this:

1. Trials will come.
2. Trials will be various.

First, James says when trials come not if they will come. James is very clear believers will face trials of many kinds. It should be expected. Not with fear but with joy. Now that seems conflicting because who rejoices over trials? But James tells us why and how we can do this.

Joy is not the absence of trials. If we think we have perfect lives or God promises us perfect lives then we lie to ourselves and any joy we experience is superficial. The truth is, we can choose joy even in the midst of trials. This is a good thing because the second lesson we learn from James is that the trails we face sometimes will be various. We see this to be true not only in our own lives but also in the lives of those who inspire us in the Bible:

Joseph faced rejection, injustice, mistreatment, and betrayal.

Moses endured an identity crisis, shame, and fear.

Naomi suffered loss, bitterness, and loneliness.

David had to deal with being overlooked, the fear of losing his life, family drama and loss.

And Job, well, Job dealt with it all!

Still, in the face of all this James tells us to count it all joy.

How do we count it all joy when we face trials like this?

James instructs us to know that the testing of our faith produces perseverance. Perseverance is the ability to wait and endure patiently. Why would the testing of our faith produce perseverance? Because our faith is in what we can't see. Faith requires us to trust God even when we have no visual or physical reason to do so. So when trials come and test our faith, we have the choice to believe God or not. When we choose to believe God and see Him show Himself faithful, it encourages us to keep the faith next time that we face a trial.

We learn to be patient, endure, and preserve because we know

God will keep His promises. If we want to maintain our joy through testing and trials there are a few things we must know:

First, we know that there is a purpose for our trials. When we know and understand that there is a reason for our trials, we don't lose our trust in God thinking He would have us go through testing for no reason. James tells us the purpose of our trials is perseverance. Knowing God does not cause our trials, but will use them for our good and His glory, helps us to better maintain our joy in Him.

Second, we know that God's truth is greater than our feelings.

During trials, we may feel alone, but God's truth says: He will never leave or forsake us. (Deuteronomy 31:6)

We may feel rejected, but God's truth says: we are His children. (1 John 3:1)

We may feel empty handed, but God's truth says: He will give us our daily bread. (Matthew 6:11)

We may feel hopeless, but God's truth says: He is the God of all hope. (Romans 15:13)

We may feel weak, but God's truth says: He is strong especially when we are weak. (2 Corinthians 12:10)

We may feel afraid and anxious, but God's truth says: He is faithful! (2 Timothy 2:13)

We must know that God will use our trials to grow us, not destroy us. The purpose of our trials are not to weaken us but to strengthen our faith. In 2 Corinthians 1:8-9 Paul says this about the trials he faced:

"We do not want you to be uninformed, brothers and sisters, about the troubles we experienced in the province of Asia. We were under great pressure, far beyond our ability to endure, so that we despaired of life itself. Indeed, we felt we had received the sentence of death. But this happened that we might not rely on ourselves but on God, who raises the dead." 2 Corinthians 1:8-9 NIV

One of the reasons for our trials is to mature us to have a persevering faith, but there's one thing we must do for that to happen. We have to let it. James tells us to:

"Let perseverance finish its work

so that you may be mature and complete, not lacking anything." – James 1:4 NIV

Trials build endurance, but we have to let them. You have to let perseverance complete its work. Don't skip the test and don't rush the trial.

David says "though I walk through the valley" (Psalm 23:4), but we want to run. We want to rush, but maturity cannot be rushed, especially spiritual maturity.

There are a few reasons why we want to rush this process:

First, we think we are already mature, but we can't grow if we don't realize we need too. There is nothing like a test to show you how little patience you have and how much you need to grow. God shows us our weakness and shortcomings, not to leave us there, but to grow us.

The second reason it's challenging to let perseverance complete its work is that the process just hurts. We run from pain, but God uses it to grow us. We can endure when we are more focused on the results of our enduring than the pain itself. Maturity takes pressure.

Growth doesn't happen when nothing happens. Even seeds have to break before they can start to grow. There is a necessary season of breaking, darkness, and making its way through obstacles that have to happen before growth can even be seen.

The last reason it is challenging to let perseverance finish its work is that we want instant gratification. Maturity takes time. No one is immediately spiritually mature once they get saved. Immediately we are justified by God, but then we also start a process called sanctification, by which God helps to mold and develop us to be and spiritually look more like His Son Jesus Christ. And that process takes time, so we need to let it.

Here's what we learn about the mature Christian who lets perseverance complete its work: this person still has joy even in the midst of trials. Where the spiritually immature may find themselves in despair and hopelessness, the mature may be hurting, uncomfortable, and even in pain but they still have joy knowing God loves them, He is with them, and everything is working out for their good and God's glory. So no matter what happens they can count it all joy.

"TRIALS BUILD *Endurance*, BUT WE HAVE TO *Let* THEM."

COUNT OTHERS MORE
Significant
THAN YOURSELVES

PHILIPPIANS 2:3

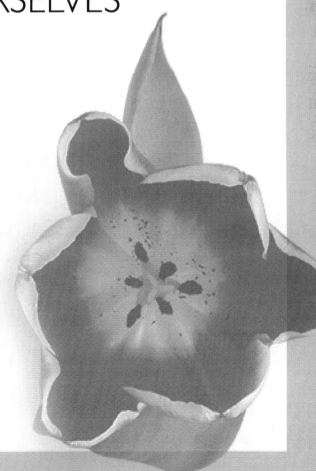

Session 4:

DO NOTHING OUT OF SELFISH AMBITION

READING

Philippians 2:1-4

FOCUS VERSE

> *"Do nothing from selfish ambition or conceit, but in humility count others more significant than yourselves." – Philippians 2:3 ESV*

KEY INSIGHT

In our hustle, busy, work work work culture we know all about ambition. Ambition is an applauded characteristic of an individual that we many times associate with success and riches. This determination to achieve is not all bad. Paul does not warn us against ambition, but selfish ambition. This is the determination to achieve only for oneself.

However, God made us for community, so we will not find true joy in working for our own desires. We may find temporary pleasure in manufacturing a life that we think we want or will make us happy but we then forfeit the more abundant life Christ offers that's greater than anything we can ask or imagine. (Ephesians 3:20)

My manufactured happiness would have been a fast-paced independent career woman quickly climbing her way up the corporate ladder. So it's funny how I've found joy in simply being home with my kids because that's what God called me to do.

Maybe for you, it is a fast-paced career, or running your own business, or being a professional athlete, or working at a 9-5, or leading a women's Bible Study. Whatever it is be ambitious about what God has called you to do, not only what you think happiness is.

We all have this idea of what we think will make us happy and we're tempted to spend our whole lives working toward that happiness. But true joy is not found in seeking happiness. True joy is found in seeking God.

Many times it's our trying to make ourselves happy that's sealing our joy, harming our relationships, and getting us off focus. We don't need to find joy when joy has already found us. A selfishly ambitious life will not lead to joy. A life spent seeking the One who gives joy will.

SESSION FOUR VIEWER GUIDE

Directions: Watch Session 4 of the "Relentless Joy" Video Bible Study series and fill in the blanks below.

There cannot be unity without
1._____.

Paul's Prescription for Unity:

I. Do nothing out of
2._____ ambition.

II. In humility, count others as more
3._____ than yourself.

III. Look to the 4._____ of others.

God made us for 5._____ so we will not find true joy in working for our own desires.

True joy is not found in seeking
6._____. True joy is found in seeking 7._____.

VIDEO NOTES:

SESSION FOUR STUDY QUESTIONS

1. Paul gives clear instruction on how the Philippians may maintain unity among themselves. Why is unity important to experiencing the joy of the Lord?

2. What are some challenges that prevent unity among Christians?

3. How does today's lesson teach us to overcome the challenges to unity discussed in the previous question?

4. How would you explain the difference between godly ambition and selfish ambition?

5. What challenges do believers face with it comes to making sure they are not selfishly ambitious?

6. How can we make sure we do nothing out of selfish ambition?

7. In what ways do we sometimes misunderstand what humility is and what it looks like in the believer's life? What does true humility look like?

8. How can our trust is God help us to look out more for the interest of others?

JOURNAL PROMPT

Write about a time you were humble or someone was humble to you.
How did that time create more unity in your life or relationships?

_____

_____

_____

_____

_____

_____

_____

_____

_____

_____

_____

_____

_____

_____

_____

_____

_____

_____

_____

_____

GOING _Deeper_ WITH YOUR LIFE BIBLE JOURNAL

Reading: Philippians 2:1-4
READ: What does Paul instruct the Philippians to do to live in unity with one another?
REFLECT: Why is humility an important part of maintaining unity?
RESPOND: How can you cultivate more unity in your relationships?
REQUEST: Pray for a clear understanding of humility and for the power to live humbly.

SESSION FOUR NOTES

HAVE THIS

Mind

AMONG YOURSELVES

WHICH IS YOURS IN

Christ Jesus

PHILIPPIANS 2:5

Session 5: HAVING THE MIND OF CHRIST

READING

Philippians 2:5-11

FOCUS VERSE

> *"Have this mind among yourselves, which is yours in Christ Jesus, who, though he was in the form of God, did not count equality with God a thing to be grasped." – Philippians 2:5-6 ESV*

KEY INSIGHT

On the verge of His gruesome crucifixion, Jesus prayed in the garden of Gethsemane. He asked God to take this cross from Him but ultimately His prayer was for God's will to be done even if it meant His death. Soon after his prayer, Judas, one of Jesus' disciples led a group of people to come and capture Jesus. In an attempt to protect Jesus, one of His disciples pulled out his sword and cut off the ear of one of the people who were there to seize Jesus. This disciple's intention was to protect his Lord. You'd think Jesus would be fine with this but listen to what Jesus says about the attack:

> *"Put your sword back into its place. For all who take the sword will perish by the sword. Do you think that I cannot appeal to my Father, and he will at once send me more than twelve legions of angels? But how then should the Scriptures be fulfilled, that it must be so?" - Matthew 26:52-54 ESV*

Jesus could have stopped the crowd coming to arrest Him. Jesus could have prevented His crucifixion but He allows it all to take place so that the scriptures may be fulfilled. What does that mean? It means Jesus came to save us. That was what the Old Testament prophesied. That God would send a Savior to the world to save us from our sins that we might be in right relationship with Him. Jesus is that Savior. So for Him to use His power to save Himself would mean our eternal condemnation. But because His mission was to save us, He humbled Himself, He controlled His power, and fulfilled the will of God that we might be saved.

It would have been easier for Jesus to save Himself. He shows more strength by not saving Himself because His rescue was one simple request away.

In Philippians Paul is telling us this is the mindset of the humble. Not what's easy but what's best. We, however, struggle with this mindset because pride tells us we'll look weak. But humility is not weakness, it's power controlled. It's the ability to keep your mouth shut when you have the perfect comeback to shut the whole argument down. It's the ability to treat the janitor with the same respect you treat the CEO. It's the ability to admit you're wrong when you really don't have to. It's the ability to give someone else the opportunity to do something you can do better.

Humility is laying down our strength, not because we're weak, but for a greater good. And if Jesus who is equal to God can humble Himself, surely should we.

SESSION FIVE VIEWER GUIDE

Directions: Watch Session 5 of the "Relentless Joy" Video Bible Study series and fill in the blanks below.

As we look to the example of Jesus we learn 3 important mindsets we must have to live humbly.

Three Mindsets of Humility:

1. Understand you don't have to do something just because you can.

Jesus could have come to 1._____ the world, but instead, He
2._____ himself for the world.

This is the mindset of the humble; not what's easy, but what's 3._____.

Humility is not weakness, it's
4._____controlled.

2. Understand everything you have is from God.

5._____ has a mindset that everything I have is from God and everything I've achieved is because God has allowed it.

People don't need to see how great we are. They need us to meet them where they are and show them how great 6._____ is.

3. Understand the value of sacrifice.

Jesus gave up His life so we could have
7._____.

VIDEO NOTES:

If we want to follow the humble example of 8._____, by pouring our lives out like Him, we must fill up on Him.

SESSION FIVE STUDY QUESTIONS

1. How does Jesus show us what true humility looks like?

2. How does Jesus' act of humility encourage you to live humbly?

3. What types of mindsets or thoughts prevent us from being humble?

4. Through the example of Jesus, we learn that humility is not a sign of weakness but power and strength. Why do you think humility is often seen as a sign of weakness?

5. Why is humility actually a sign of strength and not weakness?

6. How can we show humility when we might be better at something than someone else?

7. How can we stay humble in a society that glorifies self?

8. What are the benefits of living a humble life?

JOURNAL PROMPT

What challenges your ability to be humble? Think of Jesus's sacrifice for your salvation. How does His humility inspire you to live humbly?

_____
_____
_____
_____
_____
_____
_____
_____
_____
_____
_____
_____
_____
_____
_____
_____
_____
_____
_____
_____

GOING _Deeper_ WITH YOUR LIFE BIBLE JOURNAL

Reading: Philippians 2:5-11
READ: Whose example does Paul say we should follow?
REFLECT: Why does Jesus serve as an excellent example of a humble life?
RESPOND: How can you follow Christ's example to live humbly?
REQUEST: Pray for grace, power, and wisdom to have the humble mindset of Christ.

SESSION FIVE NOTES

WORK OUT YOUR OWN
Salvation
WITH FEAR & TREMBLING

PHILIPPIANS 2:12

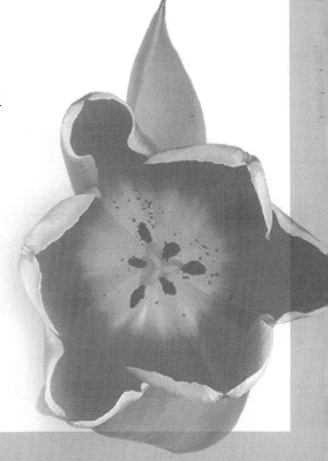

Session 6:

WORK OUT YOUR SALVATION WITH FEAR AND TREMBLING

READING

Philippians 2:12-18

FOCUS VERSE

> *"Therefore, my beloved, as you have always obeyed, so now, not only as in my presence but much more in my absence, work out your own salvation with fear and trembling, for it is God who works in you, both to will and to work for his good pleasure." – Philippians 2:12-13 ESV*

KEY INSIGHT

To work out our salvation means not to only be saved but to live saved. It means to activate our faith, and live as we believe in Christ in a way that it is evident in every area of our lives and the decisions we make. Yes, God is the one who saves us. He does that work. Our work is to live it out and take advantage of the benefits of our salvation in Christ. Before we were saved we were slaves to sin. We had no power to live for God. Through Christ, however, we now have that power but we still have to choose to use it.

We have the joy of Christ, the peace of Christ, the love of Christ. But just because we have those gifts does not mean we've actively opened them and used them.

Just because I give my child a computer to do their homework does not mean their homework automatically gets done. They must open the present, turn it on and use it. Working out our salvation does not simply mean knowing what to do to live for Christ, it's actually taking action to do it.

We do this by being obedient to God through faith. We trust Him to choose to live in the manner in which He desires.

As we work out our own salvation we are to do so, as Paul instructs, with fear and trembling. Does this mean we should walk around timid looking over our shoulder waiting for God to get us? No! Paul does not say fear here as in being scared or afraid of God. We don't need to do that. He's a good Father. Working out our salvation with fear and trembling means our obedience is out of reverence and honor to God. It's acting in such a way that shows respect for who God is.

Scary fear will not lead to obedience and this is not what God wants from us. Scary fear will only lead to behavior modification but not true heart change. As our loving Father God wants our hearts and as our Lord He wants us to take Him seriously and believe the truth about Him.

As we work out our salvation with fear and trembling we're not walking around scared of losing our salvation but we live out the salvation already granted to us.

SESSION SIX VIEWER GUIDE

Directions: Watch Session 6 of the "Relentless Joy" Video Bible Study series and fill in the blanks below.

WORK OUT YOUR OWN SALVATION

To work out our salvation means not to only be saved but to
1._____ saved.

We have the joy of Christ, the peace of Christ, the love of Christ. But just because we have those
2._____ does not mean we've actively opened them and used them.

As we work out our salvation with fear and trembling we're not walking around
3._____ of losing our salvation but we live out the salvation already granted to us.

DO ALL THINGS WITHOUT GRUMBLING OR DISPUTING

The time we waste 4._____ is time we could spend doing something about the complaint.

When we resist complaining or grumbling the scripture says we will shine as
5._____ in the world.

HOLD FAST TO THE WORD OF LIFE

Living for Christ brings 6._____. The World would distract us to think otherwise.

As we hold on to the truth of God and His
7._____, we are also holding on to our joy.

VIDEO NOTES:

SESSION SIX STUDY QUESTIONS

1. What does it mean to work out your salvation with fear and trembling?

2. In this session we learned to work out our salvation means not to only be saved but to live saved. How can we make sure we live out what we believe?

3. What are the negative effects of complaining and grumbling?

4. How can believers make sure they don't complain and argue with one another?

5. Why does Paul tell the Philippians to hold fast to the word of life?

6. How does God's Word help believers experience true joy?

JOURNAL PROMPT

Reflect on your relationship with God. Have you allowed Him to lead your life or has He taken a back seat? Why?

_____

_____

_____

_____

_____

_____

_____

_____

_____

_____

_____

_____

_____

_____

_____

_____

_____

GOING *Deeper* WITH YOUR LIFE BIBLE JOURNAL

Reading: Philippians 2:12-18
READ: What instruction does Paul give the Philippians to do?
REFLECT: Why is it important that the Philippians work out their own salvation, abstain from complaining, and hold fast to the word of life?
RESPOND: Of the instructions to the Philippians that Paul provides, which do you struggle with the most and what can you do to grow in this area?
REQUEST: Pray for wisdom and power to work out your salvation with reverence and honor to God.

SESSION SIX NOTES

A Closer Look

5 HABITS THAT LEAD TO JOY

Most people want more joy in their lives. Unfortunately many times we can confuse happiness and real joy. We then do things like grow our social media, strive to make a lot of money, work hard to look a certain way or fit in with a particular group of people. These things may make us happy if we attain them, but they do not lead to true joy. The lasting joy that our souls crave comes from God. The Bible shows us how we can experience more of God's joy in our lives with these five habits that lead to joy.

1. OBEDIENCE

The first (and I would argue maybe the most important) habit we can practice to experience more joy in our lives is obedience to God.

To some, this may seem counterproductive because many people have a flawed view of obedience. We mistakenly think obedience to God is this boring life just obeying God like mindless robots. However, the scriptures provide a freeing and more correct view of obedience, one that leads directly to joy in our lives.

In one of His last conversations with His disciples, Jesus tells them to abide in Him, abide in His Word, and abide in His love. In John 15:10-11 we read:

"If you keep my commandments, you will abide in my love, just as I have kept my Father's commandments and abide in his love. These things I have spoken to you, that my joy may be in you, and that your joy may be full." - John 15:10-11 ESV

In this verse, we see a unique connection between our obedience to Christ and experiencing His Joy.

Our obedience to God is how we abide in His love, and when we abide in His love, we experience the fullness of His Joy. God wants us to obey Him, not because He's some dictator but because it is how we experience the joy He desperately wants to give us. Proverbs 10:28 says:

"The hope of the righteous brings joy, but the expectation of the wicked will perish." - Proverbs 10:28 ESV

Obedience leads to joy, and every time we turn from Christ we turn from knowing His love and the joy that it brings. As believers, we will always have God's love and joy, but disobedience prevents us from experiencing it.

2. PRAISE

The next habit that leads to joy is praise. This too also seems counterproductive. If I don't feel joyful, I don't want to praise. But Psalm 100:1-4 says:

"Make a joyful noise to the Lord, all the earth! Serve the Lord with gladness! Come into his presence with singing! Know that the Lord, he is God! It is he who made us, and we are his; we are his people and the sheep of his pasture. Enter his gates with thanksgiving, and his courts with praise! Give thanks to him; bless his name!" - Psalms 100:1-4 ESV

As God's people, we are called to praise and thank Him. This is not a suggestion but a command. Psalm 71:23 says:

"My lips will shout for joy, when I sing praises to you; my soul also, which you have redeemed." – Psalm 71:23 ESV

From this psalmist, we see he doesn't shout for joy until after he sings praises. Sometimes praise comes before joy. Sometimes we can't wait to feel joy before we praise God.

When we praise God, we're thinking about Him and not what may be making us sad. We are then reminded that our God is greater and better than anything that has us down and because He never changes we have joy.

3. CONTENTMENT

Next, living a content life leads to joy. Contentment is a state of satisfaction. It's being happy right where you are.

One of the most popular scriptures on contentment is Philippians 4:12-13 that says:

"I know how to be brought low, and I know how to abound. In any and every circumstance, I

have learned the secret of facing plenty and hunger, abundance and need. I can do all things through him who strengthens me." - Philippians 4:12-13 ESV

The Apostle Paul had to learn contentment because contentment is a learned behavior. It's continuously realizing our feelings don't have to be led by our circumstance. Contentment helps us to appreciate what we already have. We don't need to seek happiness because we already have joy. We don't need to seek fame because we are already know by God. Because of God and who He is, we can experience the joy that comes from being content.

4. FOCUS

Next, focus leads to joy. Jesus sets this example for us in Hebrews 12:2 that says:

"Looking to Jesus, the founder and perfecter of our faith, who for the joy that was set before him endured the cross, despising the shame, and is seated at the right hand of the throne of God."
- Hebrews 12:2 ESV
Jesus was focused on His mission. Not even the stuffing He endured on the cross could take

away His joy. As we look to Him, as the scripture tells us, we find joy because He is our source of joy.

When I don't have my glasses on or contacts in everything is out of focus. I can't see clearly and what appears to be one thing to me might actually be another. In the same way, this world has a way of spiritually blurring our vision. A challenge looks impossible, and a problem seems hopeless when our focus is off. But when we focus on Jesus, our vision becomes clear. We can see He's still in control, and we can see everything is going to be okay when we have our focus right.

5. SERVING / GIVING

The final habit that leads to joy is serving and giving. 2 Corinthians 9:7 says:

"Each one must give as he has decided in his heart, not reluctantly or under compulsion, for God loves a cheerful giver." -
2 Corinthians 9:7 ESV

I know how easy it is to keep things to ourselves. Our time, money, talents, stories, and our lives are many times easier kept unshared. But we're made for more. We were made to live beyond just ourselves and impact those around us. And as we give, we also receive and what joy that will bring.

"WE DON'T HAVE TO SEEK *Happiness,*

BECAUSE WE ALREADY HAVE *Joy.*"

I TRUST IN THE
Lord

PHILIPPIANS 2:24

# Session 7: THE JOY OF BEING PRESENT

READING

Philippians 2:19-30

FOCUS VERSE

> *"I trust in the Lord that shortly I myself will come also." –*
> *Philippians 2:24 ESV*

KEY INSIGHT

Many of us would find joy right in front of us if we weren't so busy distracted with everything else. But joy is not found in distractions. Joy is found in the presence of God.

Psalm 16:11 tells us:

> *"You make known to me the path of life; in your presence there is fullness of joy; at your right hand are pleasures forevermore." -*
> *Psalm 16:11ESV*

As I've said before: we don't find joy by simply seeking happiness, we experience joy by seeking God. One of the greatest things preventing us from seeking God are all the distractions around us. We'd rather rest with a Netflix binge when we know the Prince of Peace.

We'd rather find satisfaction scrolling on our phones when we can talk to the God of the universe.

We'd rather find connection on social media when we know our Creator who knows every hair on our heads.

We'd rather find relief distracting ourselves than seeking our true Source of joy.

And if we're not distracted in the present, we're distracted with the past or the future. We can't enjoy the presence of God when we're worried about the past or anxious about the future. The Bible tells us:

> *"The steadfast love of the LORD never ceases; his mercies never come to an end; they are new every morning; great is your faithfulness." - Lamentations 3:22-23 ESV*

God's mercies are made new every morning. They are not new yesterday or tomorrow, but today. We find God in the now. In being present we can clearly see Him moving and providing in our lives right now, no matter what our "right now" looks like. We don't need to wait for joy. Joy is where God is. So let go of the distractions, wake up, be present and experience the joy of the Lord today.

SESSION SEVEN VIEWER GUIDE

Directions: Watch Session 7 of the "Relentless Joy" Video Bible Study series and fill in the blanks below.

There is nothing like 1._____, in-person time with someone.

All of the 2._____ we have that can keep us so connected is the very source of disconnection between us and those who we actually see each day.

We've unfortunately failed to realize the importance of our 3._____.

Many of us will find joy right in front of us but we're so busy 4._____ with everything else. But joy is not found in distractions. Joy is found in the presence of God.

We'd rather find 5._____ on social media when we know our Creator who knows every hair on our heads.

God's 6._____ are made new every morning. They are not new yesterday or tomorrow, but today. We find God in the 7._____.

VIDEO NOTES:

SESSION SEVEN STUDY QUESTIONS

1. Why do you think Paul greatly desired to see the Philippians?

2. Do you have a friend or family member that's been on your heart and mind that you need to reach out to and connect with? What has prevented you from doing so?

3. What are some of the most common distractions preventing people from being present in their own lives?

4. What does being present in your life look like to you?

5. Why do you think people have become more interested in social media than real human interaction?

6. In this lesson, we learned that God's mercies are made new each day. Not yesterday or tomorrow. What things can you do to ensure you are living in the present?

7. Psalm 16:11 tells us that in God's presence there is fullness of joy. How can we enter the presence of the Lord to experience more of His joy?

JOURNAL PROMPT

What things in your life keep you distracted from the presence of God?
What feelings do you experience when you feel lured to these
distractions? Why should you trust the Lord when these feelings surface?

_____

_____

_____

_____

_____

_____

_____

_____

_____

_____

_____

_____

_____

_____

_____

_____

_____

GOING *Deeper* WITH YOUR LIFE BIBLE JOURNAL

Reading: Philippians 2:19-30
READ: Who is Paul sending to the Philippians on his behalf? Who is
Epaphroditus?
REFLECT: Why does Paul desire to see the Philippians? Why is he also
sending Epaphroditus?
RESPOND: Ask the Holy Spirit to place anyone on your heart that you
need to reach out to. How can you connect with this person soon?
REQUEST: Pray for a mindset that is not distracted but present and active
in the life God has given you.

SESSION SEVEN NOTES

PUT NO *Confidence* IN THE FLESH

PHILIPPIANS 3:3

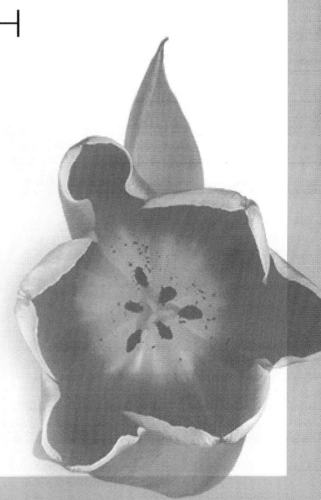

$\mathcal{S}ession$ 8: PUT NO CONFIDENCE IN THE FLESH

READING

Philippians 3:1-11

FOCUS VERSE

> "For we are the circumcision, who worship by the Spirit of God
> and glory in Christ Jesus and put no confidence in the flesh." –
> Philippians 3:3 ESV

KEY INSIGHT

As we start to take a deeper look at Philippians chapter 3 we see Paul
providing personal instruction to the Philippians as to how they should
carry themselves as believers. Of course, one of those charges is for the
Philippians to rejoice in the Lord. He says:

> "Finally, my brothers, rejoice in the Lord. To write the same things
> to you is no trouble to me and is safe for you." – Philippians 3:1
> ESV

If Paul is starting to sound a little redundant it's because he is. The
importance of the Philippians maintaining their joy in the Lord is essential.
There is also something else that Paul wants to reiterate to this church and
that is the importance of not placing their confidence in the flesh. Like
many of the early churches we see Paul write to, the Philippians were
challenged with a false Gospel that says there are certain things you need
to do to gain salvation. But that was not the true Gospel that Paul
preached to them.

Paul preached salvation, by faith, through grace alone. There is nothing we
can do to be saved. One of the most beautiful and appealing aspects of
Christianity is that Jesus already did the work. And it's important that He

did because no matter how much we try, we can't work our way to God, and we can't work off our sin. But by the grace of God, we don't have to. We simply place our faith and confidence in Christ.

The problem is, many people during Paul's time, and our time too, have an issue with this. We are tempted with pride that makes us want to work for our own salvation. We want to do it ourselves. But the true Gospel of Jesus Christ requires a humility that admits I can't do it. So Paul tells the Philippians:

> "Look out for the dogs, look out for the evildoers, look out for those who mutilate the flesh. For we are the circumcision, who worship by the Spirit of God and glory in Christ Jesus and put no confidence in the flesh." – Philippians 3:2-3 ESV

Paul is saying the Philippians did not need to take up old traditions, such as circumcision, to be saved. The Philippians were already saved because they had already accepted Christ as their Lord and Savior. Paul urges them not to put their confidence in the flesh and what they can do. They are to place their confidence in God where true joy is found. We too are called to this same faith.

SESSION EIGHT VIEWER GUIDE

Directions: Watch Session 8 of the "Relentless Joy" Video Bible Study series and fill in the blanks below.

No matter how much we try, we can't work our way to God. We can't work off our sin. But by the 1._____ of God, we don't have to. We simply place our faith and confidence in Christ.

Our temptation, however, is that we have so many 2._____ things we can place our confidence in; how many followers we have, how much money we make, how many places we've traveled, or jobs we've had.

The less confidence you have in God, the more and more you need in 3._____.

We don't realize we already have what we need in God because we are looking to sources other than God for 4._____.

Paul gains confidence because He knows 5._____.

When we place our confidence in God, there we will find 6._____ joy.

VIDEO NOTES:

SESSION EIGHT STUDY QUESTIONS

1. Paul starts Philippians 3 with the same charge for the Philippians to rejoice in the Lord? Why do you think he keeps saying this over and over?

2. During the time of Paul's writing of Philippians, there were many false Gospels going around that said one must work for salvation. The teaching of Paul, however, always made it clear that salvation is by God's grace alone through faith in Christ. Why do you think understanding the true Gospel is important to experience the joy of the Lord?

3. Why is it easier sometimes to believe we can work for our salvation instead of trusting God did all the work?

4. Towards the end of David's reign recorded in 2 Samuel 24, David makes a big mistake by counting his fighting men. Why was God disappointed that David placed his confidence in the number of his fighting men?

5. How do we place our confidence in numbers and how much we have? Why is this harmful to our experiencing joy?

6. In Philippians 3 we learn Paul has many reasons to place his confidence in his flesh. Why does he not do this and encourage believers not to place confidence in their flesh either?

JOURNAL PROMPT

Write about the last time you felt confident. Was that confidence lasting or temporary? Why or why not?

_____

_____

_____

_____

_____

_____

_____

_____

_____

_____

_____

_____

_____

_____

_____

_____

_____

_____

_____

_____

GOING _Deeper_ WITH YOUR LIFE BIBLE JOURNAL

Reading: Philippians 3:1-11

READ: What is Paul instructing the Philippians not to place their confidence in?

REFLECT: Why should we not place our confidence in the flesh?

RESPOND: How can you lean less on your ability to gain confidence and more on God's ability.

REQUEST: Pray for increased confidence in God and not to get distracted seeking the false confidence of this world.

SESSION EIGHT NOTES

I PRESS ON TOWARD THE GOAL FOR THE 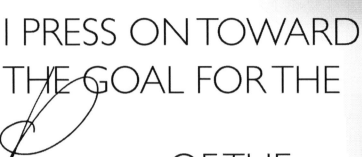*Prize* OF THE UPWARD CALL OF GOD IN *Christ Jesus*

PHILIPPIANS 3:14

Session 9:

FORGETTING WHAT LIES BEHIND AND STRAINING FORWARD

READING

Philippians 3:12-21

FOCUS VERSE

> *"Brothers, I do not consider that I have made it my own. But one thing I do: forgetting what lies behind and straining forward to what lies ahead, I press on toward the goal for the prize of the upward call of God in Christ Jesus." – Philippians 3:13-14 ESV*

KEY INSIGHT

Paul had a lot of imperfections in his past. He was once an enemy of Christians, even to the point of killing them until Jesus revealed Himself to Paul on the road to Damascus. It was then Paul converted to Christianity. The Paul we know planted much of the early church and wrote much of the New Testament. He's a saint. However, when he first converted, not everyone was convinced. Paul actually faced many opponents that constantly used his past to discredit his apostleship.

Had Paul focused on His past he would have every reason to wallow in self-pity. Instead, he's able to move forward because he does not waste time focusing on something he cannot change. In 1 Timothy 1:15-17 Paul explains it this way:

> *"The saying is trustworthy and deserving of full acceptance, that Christ Jesus came into the world to save sinners, of whom I am the foremost. But I received mercy for this reason, that in me, as the foremost, Jesus Christ might display his perfect patience as an example to those who were to believe in him for eternal life. To*

the King of the ages, immortal, invisible, the only God, be honor and glory forever and ever. Amen." – 1 Timothy 1:15-17 ESV

If we want freedom from our pasts we can't focus on our past mistakes but on God's relentless mercy. Paul is not focused on his imperfection, but God's perfect patience with Him. We can look behind, but we won't find joy there. Or we can look up to the God who redeems and restores. That is where we will find true joy.

Being free from our past isn't acting like it never happened. It's not looking back on the situation with fond memories. Freedom from our past is to look back and still see God with us, holding our hand through the darkness when at the time it didn't feel like He was there. Maybe you're not there yet, and that's okay. Still, I know that regardless of how we feel today, or what we did yesterday, God was with us even in our darkest. How do I know this? Because we're still here today. You may have been through such dark seasons where you should have lost your life, or you should have lost your mind but still, you're right here because God never let you go no matter how great the mistake, deep the rejection, or dark the valley. You are still here because God was with you. If that is the only redeeming aspect you can think of today as it pertains to your past, that God was with you, let me tell you this Beloved. That's all you need.

SESSION NINE VIEWER GUIDE

Directions: Watch Session 9 of the "Relentless Joy" Video Bible Study series and fill in the blanks below.

VIDEO NOTES:

As we walk out our faith with God, we will not be
1._____ .

One of our greatest stumbling blocks to
2._____ joy in our lives is our trying to be perfect.

The more we grow in Christ the more we realize how flawed we are yet how much more
3._____ He is.

If you're constantly focused on yourself you're
4._____ from your focus on God; who is your true source of Joy.

If we want 5._____ from our pasts we can't focus on our past mistakes but on God's relentless 6._____ .

You can look behind, but you won't find
7._____ there. Or you can look up to the God who redeems and restores.

Freedom from our past is to look back and still see God with us, holding our hand through the
8._____, when at the time it didn't feel like He was there.

Life will not be perfect here on this earth. We live in a fallen world. But praise be to God that our true 9._____ is not here.

SESSION NINE STUDY QUESTIONS

1. Paul shares that although he is not perfect he presses forward to the call of Christ Jesus. What call has God placed on all believers lives? What distracts us from this call?

2. It's easy to become overly focused on ourselves for the sake of self-development. Why is too much focus on ourselves not a good thing?

3. Paul also shares that he forgets what is behind. How do we sometimes allow our past to prevent us from experiencing the joy of the Lord?

4. Why can we let go of guilt and shame of our past to move forward in Christ?

5. We can become tempted to strive for a perfect life in order to find joy. Why is joy not found in seeking perfection?

6. Why can we have hope although our lives may not be perfect?

JOURNAL PROMPT

What's the hardest thing you've had to let go of for Christ? Why was (or is) it worth it?

_____

_____

_____

_____

_____

_____

_____

_____

_____

_____

_____

_____

_____

_____

_____

_____

_____

_____

_____

GOING *Deeper* WITH YOUR LIFE BIBLE JOURNAL

Reading: Philippians 3:12-21

READ: What does Paul do to press on toward the call of Christ on his life?

REFLECT: Why does Paul "forget what is behind?"

RESPOND: What things might you need to let go of to press forward in Christ?

REQUEST: Pray for wisdom to know when to let go and when to press forward in your life.

SESSION NINE NOTES

A Closer Look

FINDING JOY IN TIMES OF SUFFERING

*L*ast year I had the privilege of teaching adult Sunday school at my church. We had a wonderful seven weeks of learning about biblical joy. Interesting enough, session six was about maintaining joy in the midst of suffering. Most would think joy and suffering could not exist in the same person at the same time, but that's not true. Although we live in this fallen world and suffering is inevitable, as believers we also have the gift of joy as a fruit of the Spirit (Galatians 5:22-23).

This gift is not dependent on our current circumstance but the fact that our Heavenly Father gave it to us. Still, it's a challenging concept to grasp as I've learned that many Christians sometimes have misconceptions about suffering. We accept Christ thinking all the benefits of a relationship with Him and the fruits of the Spirit exempt us from suffering. This thinking, however, is harmful because guess what? Believers still suffer on this side of eternity.

Now, this does not mean God has forgotten us. It means He's with us during both the good and the bad. Actually, suffering itself provides gifts for the believer that you may find encouraging. Here are five gifts that result from seasons of suffering.

I. CLOSENESS TO GOD

"The Lord is near to the brokenhearted and saves the crushed in spirit. Many are the afflictions of the righteous, but the Lord delivers him out of them all." - Psalms 34:18-19 ESV

Many times we believe that the presence of suffering means the absence of God. On the contrary! When God's children are suffering the Bible tells us He is then close to us, not far away. God is not the cause of our suffering and does not delight in our pain. He does not take our hurt lightly. As I would run to my children's side even at the smallest scrap of the knee, surely our Heavenly Father is with us when our hearts are crushed, and despair has taken over.

The gift of God's presence is not dependent on how well our life is going but on His love for us. And since He loves us all the time, even sending His Son to die on our behalf, He will always be with us during the good and the bad. One of God's greatest gifts to us is His presence. Though we sometimes have to walk through the valley, we do not walk alone.

"Even though I walk through the valley of the shadow of death, I will fear no evil, for you are with me; your rod and your staff, they comfort me." - Psalms 23:4 ESV

2. INCREASED FAITH

"In all this, you greatly rejoice, though now for a little while you may have had to suffer grief in all kinds of trials. These have come so that the proven genuineness of your faith—of greater worth than gold, which perishes even though refined by fire—may result in praise, glory and honor when Jesus Christ is revealed." - 1 Peter 1:6-7 NIV

Suffering surely does test our faith. It's easy to believe our God is a good Father when things are going well. But can we uphold this faith when it feels like we are going through the fires of life?

The Apostle Peter in the verse above encourages believers that the development of our faith during suffering is of great worth. Suffering causes us to cling to God like never before, granting us the ability to see God's strength, love, and power in our lives like never before.

The most defining faith moments in my life have been in times of suffering, giving me a clear revelation of God and His love for me that strengthened my trust in Him.

3. ABILITY TO COMFORT OTHERS

"Blessed be the God and Father of our Lord Jesus Christ, the Father of mercies and God of all comfort, who comforts us in all our affliction, so that we may be able to comfort those who are in any affliction, with the comfort with which we ourselves are comforted by God." - 2 Corinthians 1:3-4 ESV

When we're suffering, it's easy to get caught up in our own struggles and focus solely on our own issues. However, we don't have to search far to find others suffering just like us and, many times, facing much more difficulties. What our suffering does is grant us the ability to truly understand the hurting world around us with compassion, care, and empathy.

When I'm suffering, I find great encouragement from those who've walked the same or a similar path. It's a testimony that if God brought them through, He can do so from me as well. This gives me great comfort. In my suffering, I too can offer this same gift of comfort to others.

4. FELLOWSHIP WITH CHRIST

"Indeed, I count everything as loss because of the surpassing worth of knowing Christ Jesus my Lord. For his sake I have suffered the loss of all things and count them as rubbish, in order that I may gain Christ and be found in him, not having a righteousness of my own that comes from the law, but that which comes through faith in Christ, the righteousness from God that depends on faith— that I may know him and the power of his resurrection, and may share his sufferings, becoming like him in his death, that by any means possible I may

attain the resurrection from the dead." - Philippians 3:8-11 ESV

One of the most unique aspects of the Christian faith is that our Savior suffered and overcame. Yes, Jesus was sinless, but He lived a tough life.

He knew all about suffering. So when we suffer we can know that not only does our God care, He understands. In our suffering, we gain more fellowship with Christ that the Apostle Paul describes in Philippians 3:8-11 as far more significant than everything he was able to attain in the flesh.

What a gift that our God does not turn His back on those who suffer because He too suffered.

5. ETERNAL PERSPECTIVE

"I consider that our present sufferings are not worth comparing with the glory that will be revealed in us." - Romans 8:18 NIV

Our sorrow here on earth is temporary, whereas the benefits of the Gospel will last forever. This is the hope and gift for the one who is suffering. Our present suffering is not the end. This too shall pass. This fallen earth is not our final destination.

We are passing through and our time here is temporary. There is work to do and God has His purposes for having us here but the Bible tells us this is not where we hold citizenship. Philippians 3:20-21 reminds us of this:

"But our citizenship is in heaven. And we eagerly await a Savior from there, the Lord Jesus Christ, who, by the power that enables him to bring everything under his control, will transform our lowly bodies so that they will be like his glorious body." -Philippians 3:20-21 NIV

Our suffering is a constant reminder that this is not the end.

Because of the Gospel of Jesus Christ, we are gifted the hope of an eternal perspective even when we are hurting – especially when we are hurting. During seasons of suffering our fear is we will be in pain forever, but the Gospel gives us greater perspective on suffering and pain.

No one wants to suffer, but praise be to God Our Father that this is not the end. And even while we suffer here on this side of eternity, we have the gifts of closeness to God, increased faith, comfort, fellowship with Christ, and hope for a better tomorrow. These eternal gifts ensure we always have something to be joyful about.

"THE GIFT OF GOD'S *Presence* IS NOT DEPENDENT ON HOW WELL OUR LIFE IS GOING, BUT ON HIS *Love* FOR US."

*This article originally appeared on iBelieve.com at https://www.ibelieve.com/health-beauty/how-can-suffering-be-good-5-ways-suffering-is-an-unexpected-gift.html

REJOICE IN THE

Lord

ALWAYS; AGAIN
I WILL SAY,

Rejoice

PHILIPPIANS 4:4

Session 10:

THE JOY OF THE LORD IS YOUR STRENGTH

READING

Philippians 4:1-4

FOCUS VERSE

> *"Rejoice in the Lord always; again I will say, rejoice." – Philippians 4:4 ESV*

KEY INSIGHT

When we don't know how things will turn out it may feel impossible to rejoice. This is why Paul says to do so in the Lord, not your circumstance. Your circumstance will not grant you strength or joy. Actually, your circumstance may very well be the thing stealing your strength and joy but praise be to God He is our source and not what has or will happen to us. God is an everlasting source of joy and strength, and the more we depend on Him, the more strength and joy we will experience. The Bible tells us:

> *"The joy of the Lord is your strength." – Nehemiah 8:10 ESV*

When we truly understand that God is joy and He is not this mean, angry, and distant God, but believe that He will help us in our time of need, we are strengthened.

"The joy of the Lord is your strength" means because God rejoices over you, He will give you the strength that you need to live the life that He's calling you to live.

Not understanding this truth presented a great challenge for me while I was in college because when I was convicted of a mistake or sin I would get discouraged and frustrated. Sometimes I'm still tempted to fall into that same pattern of thinking but now I know better.

I know that if God is revealing some brokenness or sin in my life it's because He has every intention of helping me. So now when I'm convicted I don't feel sad. I actually feel happy that God loves and rejoices over me enough not to leave me in my sin. Even more, I see it as a call to cling closer to Him because I know He is about to strengthen me in an area I'm weak. It is His joy that will do it, not my attempt to better myself on my own. We can't do it on our own and we can't change our own hearts. Only God can do that and because of His joy, we can trust that He will.

SESSION TEN VIEWER GUIDE

Directions: Watch Session 10 of the "Relentless Joy" Video Bible Study series and fill in the blanks below.

As we focus less on proving ourselves
1._____ and more on living as God desires us to, the more unity we will find in our relationships.

No matter the uncertainty, no matter the strife, no matter the sickness, no matter the anxiety or worries, or fear Paul says to "rejoice." Not in these things but in the
2._____!

When we don't know how things will turn out it may feel 3._____ to rejoice. This is why Paul says to do so in the Lord, not your
4._____.

God is an everlasting source of joy and
5._____.

God does not reveal our shortcomings to us for the sake of just doing it. He convicts us when He has every intention of providing the wisdom, discernment, and strength to
6._____ us.

We can't change our own 7._____.
Only God can do that and because of His joy, we can trust that He will.

VIDEO NOTES:

SESSION TEN STUDY QUESTIONS

1. Paul encourages two women in the Church at Philippi to "agree in the Lord" when it appears they are in disagreement. How can we "agree in the Lord" with those whom we may disagree?

2. Why does agreement in the Lord help promote unity in relationships?

3. Is there an area in your life where you need to constantly be reminded to rejoice in the Lord? What is it and why?

4. What do you think it means when the Bible says "the joy of the Lord is your strength"? (Nehemiah 8:10)

5. Why can we trust God to strengthen us when we make mistakes and sin?

JOURNAL PROMPT

How do you respond to disagreements? Do your actions align with how God would want you to respond? Why or why not?

_____

_____

_____

_____

_____

_____

_____

_____

_____

_____

_____

_____

_____

_____

_____

_____

_____

_____

_____

_____

_____

GOING _Deeper_ WITH YOUR LIFE BIBLE JOURNAL

Reading: Philippians 4:1-4
READ: What does Paul tell Euodia and Syntyche to do?
REFLECT: Why is it important that they "agree in the Lord"?
RESPOND: How can believers promote unity by agreeing in the Lord?
REQUEST: Ask the Lord to reveal any conflict in your relationships and for healing and unity.

SESSION TEN NOTES

DO NOT BE

Anxious

ABOUT ANYTHING

PHILIPPIANS 4:6

$\mathcal{S}ession$ 11:

DO NOT BE ANXIOUS ABOUT ANYTHING

READING

Philippians 4:5-9

FOCUS VERSE

> *"Do not be anxious about anything, but in everything by prayer and supplication with thanksgiving let your requests be made known to God." – Philippians 4:6 ESV*

KEY INSIGHT

In light of the challenges Paul is facing and the worries the Philippians have for him, Paul commands (not suggests) that they not be anxious about anything. Still, they had a lot to worry about. Being persecuted, strife among believers and the uncertainty of Paul's future are just a few of the things they could have worried about. In light of all their anxieties Paul reasons: Why worry when you can pray.

Worry accomplishes nothing, but prayer to God is taking your issues to Someone who can actually do something about them. So we're called to pray about everything. Not just some things but everything.

If you can worry about it, you should be praying about it.

Although we are to pray with supplication, meaning telling God what we what Him to do, we are also to pray with thanksgiving ensuring we maintain a focus on what He's already done for us. As we do this Paul says:

"And the peace of God, which surpasses all understanding, will guard your hearts and your minds in Christ Jesus." - Philippians 4:7 ESV

God will cover our hearts and minds. He will guide our feelings and thoughts. Anxiety is a feeling and as God covers our hearts, He protects us from being anxious. At the same time He also wants to protect our minds so Paul says:

"Finally, brothers, whatever is true, whatever is honorable, whatever is just, whatever is pure, whatever is lovely, whatever is commendable, if there is any excellence, if there is anything worthy of praise, think about these things." - Philippians 4:8 ESV

Many times we don't experience joy because we don't control our thoughts. However, our thoughts have a great influence on our feelings and lead our actions.

Paul gives a laundry list of things to think on; what's commendable, excellent, praiseworthy and more. I love that he first says, think on what is true.

A lot of the thoughts that we allow in our heads that lead to anxiety and prevent us from experiencing joy just aren't even true.

If we think God is mad at us or He doesn't really love us, that's just not even true. These are the anxious thoughts that we need to throw away. I challenge you. Take a mental inventory of your thoughts, write them down and ask, "Is this even true?" If it's not true let it go. If it is, pray about it, and give it to God.

SESSION ELEVEN VIEWER GUIDE

Directions: Watch Session 11 of the "Relentless Joy" Video Bible Study series and fill in the blanks below.

When we trust Christ is near there is no need to be 1._____. We have the freedom to let God fight our 2._____.

Why worry when you can 3._____.

If you can 4._____ about it you should be praying about it.

Many times we don't experience joy because we don't control our 5._____.

A lot of the thoughts that we allow in our heads that lead to anxiety and prevent us from experiencing joy just aren't even 6._____.

We won't be perfect but we should be 7._____.

VIDEO NOTES:

SESSION ELEVEN STUDY QUESTIONS

1. Why does Paul tell the Philippians not to be anxious?

2. What does Paul instruct the Philippians to do instead of being anxious?

3. Why is thanksgiving important in fighting anxiety?

4. Why is prayer important in our fight against anxiety?

5. What happens when we pray and release our anxieties to God?

6. Why are our thoughts so important when it comes to fighting anxiety?

7. What types of thoughts lead to more anxiety?

8. What types of thoughts help to fight anxiety?

JOURNAL PROMPT

Write about what is currently making you anxious. Then write why you can trust God with these issues?

_____

_____

_____

_____

_____

_____

_____

_____

_____

_____

_____

_____

_____

_____

_____

_____

_____

_____

_____

_____

GOING *Deeper* WITH YOUR LIFE BIBLE JOURNAL

Reading: Philippians 4:5–9
READ: What does Paul tell the Philippians to do instead of being anxious?
REFLECT: Why do Paul's instructions lead to a less anxious life?
RESPOND: What can you personally do more of to fight worry and anxiety in your life?
REQUEST: Pray for God's strength and wisdom to fight worry and anxiety with thanksgiving, prayer, and godly thinking.

SESSION ELEVEN NOTES

I CAN DO

All Things

THROUGH HIM WHO

STRENGTHES ME.

PHILIPPIANS 4:13

Session 12:

I CAN DO ALL THINGS THROUGH HIM WHO STRENGTHENS ME

READING

Philippians 4:10-23

FOCUS VERSE

> *"I know how to be brought low, and I know how to abound. In any and every circumstance, I have learned the secret of facing plenty and hunger, abundance and need. I can do all things through him who strengthens me." – Philippians 4:12-13 ESV*

KEY INSIGHT

As Paul closes his letter to the Philippians we learn that one of the most important keys to his joy is contentment. Here's what I found really interesting about Paul's comments on his contentment – it's something he had to learn in both seasons of plenty and seasons of lack.

We expect to put in a lot of effort to find contentment in low seasons. On the other hand, we think that contentment comes automatically in up and happy seasons, but it doesn't.

Contentment is being satisfied with what you have. The problem with us is our desires shift and change. We can spend years praying for one thing and once we get it we're on to focusing on the next thing we don't have.

So contentment is the learned practice of looking at what you have and trusting God that it's enough in whatever season you are facing. It's rejecting the lie that I need "this" or "that" to experience joy.

Paul lets us in on a little secret. The strength we need to practice a life of contentment is found in Christ. It's a life that constantly leans on Jesus for joy and not our circumstance. When we think about the roots behind our desires; we many times already have what we're looking for in Christ.

We may be chasing man's approval, but we're already accepted by God.

We may strive for a higher paycheck when the God of the universe is our provider.

We may do all crazy kinds of diets to feel good about ourselves when we're already made in the image of God.

The things we chase after to find contentment are already ours in Christ. Paul is done chasing after these things as he's found all he needs in Christ who will strengthen him in any season.

SESSION TWELVE VIEWER GUIDE

Directions: Watch Session 12 of the "Relentless Joy" Video Bible Study series and fill in the blanks below.

Contentment is being satisfied with what you
1._____ .

We can spend years 2._____ for one thing and once we get it we're on to focusing on the next thing we don't have.

Contentment is the learned
3._____ of looking at what you have and trusting God that it's enough.

The strength we need to practice a content life is found in 4._____ .

The thought that we can't be happy until we have "this" or "that" is the very thing that will rob our 5._____ .

We must remember God is our
6._____ , as we give, He supplies.

The joyful giver is joyful because they know everything they have is
7._____ God and everything they give is 8._____ God.

Because of His grace, we can truly live a life full of 9._____ joy.

VIDEO NOTES:

SESSION TWELVE STUDY QUESTIONS

1. Why was Paul content?

2. Why do you think Paul had to learn how to be content?

3. Where did Paul's strength come from?

4. What challenges do we face when it comes to living a content life? Why is it so hard to be content sometimes?

5. Paul says the Philippian's giving was a "fragrant offering" that was "pleasing to God."(Philippians 4:18) Why do you think our giving pleases God?

6. Why does giving produce joy in our lives?

JOURNAL PROMPT

Write down the things you feel you need but don't have yet. Then write how God is still providing for you in spite of what you don't yet have.

_____

_____

_____

_____

_____

_____

_____

_____

_____

_____

_____

_____

_____

_____

_____

_____

_____

_____

_____

_____

_____

_____

_____

GOING _Deeper_ WITH YOUR LIFE BIBLE JOURNAL

Reading: Philippians 4:10-23
READ: What secret does Paul share with the Philippians?
REFLECT: Why is Paul content?
RESPOND: How can you be more content with what you have?
REQUEST: Pray for a content heart that thanks God for what you have.

SESSION TWELVE NOTES

5 HABITS THAT STEAL YOUR JOY

As important as it is to know what habits help us to experience joy, it is just as important to know what habits prevent joy. I call these habits joy killers. These are attitudes, behaviors, and action that will stop you from being able to experience the joy of the Lord in your life. The mistake that I think a lot of us make with these joy killers is that we don't always recognize when we're doing them. However, as we take a brief look through the book of Philippians, we learn what's killing our joy

1. UNRESOLVED CONFLICT

Our first joy killer is unresolved conflict. I love how Paul addresses this issue in Philippians when his rivals attempt to preach the gospel with the purpose to harm him and make matters worse for him. Instead of growing resentful and vindictive he chooses to remain positive and keep a perspective that helps him to keep his joy. In Philippians 1:17-18 we read:

"The former proclaim Christ out of selfish ambition, not sincerely but thinking to afflict me in my imprisonment. What then? Only that in every way, whether in pretense or truth, Christ is proclaimed, and in that I rejoice."
– Philippians 1:17-18 ESV

Unresolved conflict steals our joy. Conflict will come but when we let it fester and turn into bitterness, prolonged anger, and resentment it prevents us from experiencing joy. Paul would have none of it. Did he have opponents? Yes. Did they disagree? Absolutely! Did their actions cause him harm? You bet! That was their intention. Paul could have been petty and tried to get them back, or get revenge, but He refused to allow their actions to control his reactions.

In the face of all this conflict and hate, Paul says "what then?" Their actions can't take away his joy, his salvation, or his purpose. People may steal your money; they may waste your time, they may cause

119

you discomfort and even pain but all that is going to pass away anyway. Our life is but a vapor. Pauls' eternal perspective allowed him to realize anything someone took from him on this earth did not compare to what was his in heaven.

How do we overcome unresolved conflict in our lives?

1. The first way we overcome unresolved conflict is to admit how we feel. We need to understand that it's okay to be angry. There are so many people that are lacking joy because they are angry but don't want to admit it. The Bible tells us to, "not sin in your anger" (Ephesians 4:26). It does not say "do not be angry." If we can't admit our anger, we can never process through it, and that's when it grows into bitterness, rage, and sin.

2. The second way we overcome unresolved conflict is to open up and communicate. First, we can pour out our hearts to God and let Him know how we feel. Second, if you can, let your offender know how you feel with the intention of reconciliation. People won't always know what you're thinking and they may not realize they offended you.

3. The last way we overcome unresolved conflict is to forgive. Forgiveness is the key that can unlock God's joy in your life. Ephesians 4:31-32 says:

"Let all bitterness and wrath and anger and clamor and slander be put away from you, along with all malice. Be kind to one another, tenderhearted, forgiving one another, as God in Christ forgave you." – Ephesians 4:31-32 ESV

We have joy because Christ forgave us and as we are called to be imitators of God, we are to forgive others as well. Not as a pass to them (God is the final judge) but as the way that we find healing and joy.

2. COMPARISON / ENVY

Our next joy killer is comparison and envy. As we continue in Philippians where we left off with Paul's opponents preaching to harm him, we learn they are doing it out of rivalry. They were envious of Paul and thought to make a competition of the Gospel.

They were jealous of Paul's ministry which doesn't even make any sense because if two people are preaching the Gospel of Jesus Christ, they are on the same team. If all the glory is going to God, where is there room for envy?

This lets us know, these particular opponents may have preached the Gospel, but their hearts were self-serving. So when they go out and see the success of Paul, they start comparing themselves to him and become envious.

Envy makes us feel less than, inadequate, and not enough. How can you feel joyful if you're feeling all those things? You can't. So if we want to experience joy, we must let go of comparing ourselves to others.

How do we rid ourselves of unhealthy comparison and envy?

1. First, realize what God has for you is for you. God only needed one Paul, and He didn't need any knockoffs. He only needs one you, but you can't do you if you're trying to be like someone else.

2. The second way to rid ourselves of comparison and envy is to set boundaries. We can do this by stop looking at what everyone else is doing. We tempt ourselves to get upset about the highlights of someone's life, and we don't even know the back story. How foolish Paul's rivals were to be jealous of him. They wanted his reach, but they didn't want his suffering. Would they be willing to travel the road to Damascus? Probably not. Paul wasn't always an apostle to the gentiles. He was once a zealous killer of Christians until the Lord stopped him in his tracts and called Paul to Himself.

But the Lord said to him, "Go, for he is a chosen instrument of mine to carry my name before the Gentiles and kings and the children of Israel. For I will show him how much he must suffer for the sake of my name." – Acts 9:15-16 ESV

Don't be envious of someone especially when you don't know what challenges they've faced.

3. The last way to avoid envy is to understand that not everyone is called to do the same thing. Even more, no one person is called to do everything. Romans 12:6-8 makes this clear:

"Having gifts that differ according to the grace given to us, let us use them: if prophecy, in proportion to our faith; if service, in our serving; the one who teaches, in his teaching; the one who exhorts, in his exhortation;

the one who contributes, in generosity; the one who leads, with zeal; the one who does acts of mercy, with cheerfulness". – Romans 12:6-8 ESV

To stop comparison and envy from stealing our joy, we must seek God, not others for our gifts and purposes.

God gives each person unique gifts specific to what He has purposed for them to accomplish. The only way to know what those gifts are and to fulfill the purpose He has given us is to seek Him, not how someone else is doing it. When we become clear on this, we have no reason to be jealous or envious and make more room for joy in our lives.

3. COMPLAINING

Our next joy killer is complaining. Paul explicitly tells the Philippians not to complain to maintain their joy.

"Do all things without grumbling or disputing, that you may be blameless and innocent, children of God without blemish in the midst of a crooked and twisted generation, among whom you shine as lights in the world." – Philippians 2:14-15 ESV

When you complain you look no different from the world. Complaining is easy, but God calls believers to a higher standard when it comes to how we use our mouths. We should use our words to be thankful and to build up, not tear down. Complaining tears down because it only focuses on the negative which prevents us from being thankful. You cannot complain and be grateful at the same time.

4. PRIDE

Our next joy killer is pride. Focusing only on yourself is a sure way to lose your joy. We were made for community and find joy in living beyond ourselves to meet the needs of others. Instead, we're tempted to work and strive to accomplish more and more. But Paul tells believers not to "do nothing out of selfish ambition" (Philippians 2:3) and not to place their confidence in the flesh (Philippians 3:3) or what they can do on their own.

When we try to do everything on our own, we get frustrated and lose joy because:

1. We can't.
2. We were made for community.

3. God's strength is more significant than our strength.

In 2 Corinthians 12:10 Paul says:

"For the sake of Christ, then, I am content with weaknesses, insults, hardships, persecutions, and calamities. For when I am weak, then I am strong." – 2 Corinthians 12:10 ESV

When we are prideful and think we can do everything on our own, we forfeit God's strength in our lives.

5. ANXIETY

Our last joy killer is a big one: anxiety. Paul makes this really clear for the Philippians: Do not be anxious. This is not a suggestion or a good idea. When it comes to anxiety Paul's advice is, just don't do it.

"Do not be anxious about anything, but in everything by prayer and supplication with thanksgiving let your requests be made known to God. And the peace of God, which surpasses all understanding, will guard your hearts and your minds in Christ Jesus." – Philippians 4:6-7 ESV

Anxiety steals space in our hearts and mind where God's peace should be. In turn, it always takes our joy. Instead of being anxious we should be prayerful. Instead of worrying, we should be thankful. This is how we overcome anxiety to live the joyful life that is our in Christ.

FINAL THOUGHTS

As we conclude our study of Philippians Paul has provided us with priceless wisdom on how to practically experience the joy of the Lord. We have learned to be thankful, not to complain, pray, not to be anxious, be content, focus on Jesus, be humble, think on good things, and so much more. It's a lot to keep up with which I way I love that Paul says:

> "What you have learned and received and heard and seen in me—practice these things, and the God of peace will be with you." - Philippians 4:9 ESV

We won't be perfect but we should be practicing. We can make the effort every day to do all the things we've learned in this study over and over again. That's what practice is.

Paul's instructions for a joyous life are not a "set it and forget it" type of thing. They are what we wake up every day and intentionally do. They will not come naturally most of the time. We have to do them over and over again and build up our spiritual muscles.

I don't want you to be discouraged as you go and do what you've learned from this study, especially if you find yourself falling back in worry or negative thinking. But through the intentional effort to do what you've learned over and over and over again without giving up, you will get it.

My son understands the concept of pushing a ball into the air to get it through the hoop to make a basket. Yet, he has not come to the point where he consistently makes a basket when he tries. Although he knows what to do, his muscles aren't strong enough yet to consistently carry it out. But the more he practices, even if he doesn't make a shot, the more his shooting muscle is being built. So when we see a whole bunch of missed shots it's easy to get discouraged. However, what we don't see is the muscle being built every time he attempts a shot which will eventually lead to actual shots in the future.

We know we need not worry, we know we need to pray, we know we need to think positive, and we know what we need to do in our walk with God. After this study, we know what we need to do to experience the joy of the Lord. Still, it's not going to happen overnight just because we know it. We have to practice it. Every time we practice these things we get stronger even if it doesn't look like it. So my final encouragement to you is to not get discouraged, keep going, and keep practicing at the joyful life that is yours in Christ.

Until our next study,

Christina

Bonus Activity

DR. JOY

Directions: After reading the article "5 Habits Killing Your Joy" you have officially earned the title of Dr. Joy. Dr. Joy receives letters from people all around the world who have lost their joy. Your job is to diagnose their joy killer and prescribe a course of action to help your patients get their joy back.

PATIENT 1: KATHY

Dear Dr. Joy,

I have absolutely no joy in my life. It seems like life is passing me by, and I'm just not where I thought I would be in life. Every time I'm on Instagram I see my friends traveling, having babies, getting married, finding new jobs, and earning more money. None of that seems to be happening for me, and I keep thinking it's because something is wrong with me. Why am I not moving forward in life like they are? I just want to live my best life, but I'm nowhere close. Please help!

Sincerely,

Kathy

Diagnosis: What is Kathy's joy killer?

_____

_____

Prescription: What does Kathy need to do to fight this joy killer and regain her joy?

_____

_____

_____

_____

DR. JOY

PATIENT 2: GRETCHEN

Dear Dr. Joy,

I am having a tough time finding joy in my life right now. I am struggling to heal from past hurt from my mom when I was a child. I really want to have a good relationship with her, but every time I see her, she says something that reminds me of the past and rubs me the wrong way. I figure she did her best raising me, but there are some things she did and said that still hurt me to this day. I'm conflicted because I want a healthy happy relationship with her, but she makes me so unhappy. I feel bad because she's my mom and I feel like we should have a better relationship, but there are some things she's done that I just can't let go. This relationship is killing my joy. Please help!

Signed,

Gretchen

Diagnosis: What is Gretchen's joy killer?

_____

_____

Prescription: What does Gretchen need to do to fight this joy killer and regain her joy?

_____

_____

_____

_____

DR. JOY

PATIENT 3: KAREN

Dear Dr. Joy

I have no joy because nothing in my life is going right. My commute to work is ridiculous and now that school is back in it takes me twice as long to get to work. My husband is no good and always leaves his shoes in the middle of the floor and lays his dirty clothes next to the clothes hamper. Is it that hard to put the dirty clothes IN the hamper??? I work in customer service, and our clients are so rude, always asking me to do things for them. Can't they do it themselves? I wish I had more money so I could quit. Ugh! Just as I'm writing this, I broke my nail! I knew I shouldn't have written this letter to you. You see! Nothing in my life is going right.

Help!

Karen

Diagnosis: What is Karen's joy killer?

_____

_____

Prescription: What does Karen need to do to fight this joy killer and regain her joy?

_____

_____

_____

_____

DR. JOY

PATIENT 4: JENNIFER

Dr. Joy,

I really need help. I am afraid of everything. I'm always looking over my shoulder waiting for something terrible to happen. I turn on the news and see all the bad things taking place, and I feel so discouraged and scared. I have a good life, but I feel like I'm waiting for my luck to run out. I'm worried something bad is going to happen and I have no joy. I don't want to live like this but how can I not be afraid with everything bad going on around us?

In need of help,

Jennifer

Diagnosis: What is Jennifer's joy killer?

_____

_____

Prescription: What does Jennifer need to do to fight this joy killer and regain her joy?

_____

_____

_____

_____

DR. JOY

PATIENT 5: SALLY

Dear Dr. Joy,

I am an extremely successful self-made businesswoman. I have made for myself lots of money and have a lot to be proud of. I grew up poor and promised myself never to be poor again, and I've achieved just that. There's just one thing. I'm not happy. I have no joy. I can make money, achieve great success, I'm popular and can date any man I want. I am confident in myself and my ability to achieve anything but every morning when I wake up I look at the ceiling and feel this emptiness in my soul. I know something is missing and I don't know how to achieve it myself.

Sincerely,

Dr. Sally Jenkins, Esq.

Diagnosis: What is Sally's joy killer?

_____

_____

Prescription: What does Sally need to do to fight this joy killer and regain her joy?

_____

_____

_____

_____

Answer Guide: 1. Comparison / Envy 2. Unresolved Conflict 3. Complaining 4. Anxiety 5. Pride

RELENTLESS *Joy* VIDEO GUIDE ANSWER KEY

SESSION ONE: 1. Partnership 2. Good Work 3. Peace 4. Grace 5. Discriminate 6. Shortcomings 7. Joyful 8. Praise 9. Glory 10. Best.

SESSION TWO: 1. Purpose 2. For Christ 3. Fear 4. Proclaimed 5. Fight 6. Competition 7. Right 8. Joy

SESSION THREE: 1. Purpose 2. Joy 3. Want 4. Sufficient 5. Hope 6. Wrong 7. United 8. Truth 9. Gift 10. Gospel

SESSION FOUR: 1. Humility 2. Selfish 3. Significant 4. Interest 5. Community 6. Happiness 7. God.

SESSION FIVE: 1. Rule 2. Sacrificed 3. Best 4. Power 5. Humility 6. God 7. Eternal Life 8. Jesus

SESSION SIX: 1. Live 2. Gifts 3. Scared 4. Complaining 5. Lights 6. Joy 7. Word

SESSION SEVEN: 1. Face-to-face 2. Technology 3. Presence 4. Distracted 5. Connection 6. Mercies 7. Now.

SESSION EIGHT: 1. Grace 2. Superficial 3. Man 4. Confidence 5. Jesus 6. True

SESSION NINE: 1. Perfect 2. Experiencing 3. Gracious 4. Distracted 5. Freedom 6. Mercy 7. Joy 8. Darkness 9. Citizenship.

SESSION TEN: 1. Right 2. Lord 3. Impossible 4. Circumstance 5. Strength 6. Change 7. Heart.

SESSION ELEVEN: 1. Defensive 2. Battles 3. Pray 4. Worry 5. Thoughts 6. True 7. Practicing

SESSION TWELVE: 1. Have 2. Praying 3. Practice 4. Christ 5. Joy 6. Provider 7. From 8. For 9. Relentless

HOW TO STUDY THE *Bible* USING
THE 4 "R"s BIBLE STUDY METHOD

The 4 "R"s Bible Study Method was created to help you get the most out of your time in God's Word in the simplest way possible. Find questions that align with our 4 "R"s Bible Study method at the end of each session. To make this as simple as possible for you, we've created the LIFE Bible Journal that guides you through each of the 4 "R"s every time you study. Get your LIFE Bible Journal at www.thebelovedboutiue.com to see how life-changing Bible Study can be!

1. READ

As you read your selected scripture for study you'll want to ask yourself the question, "what is the scripture saying?" In the "READING" section record what scriptural passage you will be reading for your study. As you read, there are a few things you'll want to write down. First, write out any key verses that particularly stick out to you. You'll find a "KEY VERSE" section where you can write down this key verse. Next, you'll want to see if you can paraphrase what the scripture is saying in your own words, to make sure you're truly grasping an understanding of the text. And finally, take note of the who, what, when, where and why of the text.

2. REFLECT

After you've read the scripture, you'll then want to REFLECT. Ask yourself the question, "what does this scripture mean?" This is where you will draw out the lessons that are meant to be learned from the text. As you reflect on the scripture you'll want to write down any promises to believe, principles to live by, or commands to follow. By reflecting on God's Word in this way, you're digging deeper into the text to gain a greater meaning.

3. RESPOND

Once you've taken time to reflect, you will then want to RESPOND to the scripture. You're asking yourself, "What can I practically do to live out what I've learned?" One reason we read God's Word is so that we can be changed by its truth. So once you've learned from the scripture you're studying, make a plan to do what it says. When we reflect on the Word we learn WHAT we need to do. However, as we respond to the Word, we discover HOW we can practically do it.

4. REQUEST

Reading and studying the Bible is much easier than actually living it out. This is why the last "R" stands for REQUEST. Request means we pray to God for the help and strength that only He can provide. After you study it is important to pray over what you've learned. Many call this "praying the scriptures". Use what you've learned from your study, to guide your prayers. The life change that studying God's word offers doesn't come from simply reading the word alone. It comes from inviting God into our hearts to enable us to live out what we've learned to be true. So seal in the truths that you've learned, by praying over what you've studied.

THE LIFE BIBLE JOURNAL IS AVAILABLE AT:
WWW.THEBELOVEDBOUTIQUE.COM

REFERENCES

Guzik, David. "Study Guide for Philippians 1-4." Blue Letter Bible. 21 Feb, 2017. Web. 21 Feb, 2019. <https://www.blueletterbible.org/Comm/guzik_david/>.

Henry, Matthew. "Commentary on Philippians 1-4." Blue Letter Bible. 1 Mar, 1996. Web. 21 Feb, 2019. <https://www.blueletterbible.org/Comm/mhc/>.

Baker, Kenneth, editor. NIV Study Bible. Zondervan, 2002.

Carson, D. A., and Douglas J. Moo. An Introduction to the New Testament. Zondervan, 2005.

WWW.BELOVEDWOMEN.ORG/BIBLESTUDY

ABOUT *Beloved Women*

Beloved Women is a 501(c)3 non-profit with the mission to encourage, equip, and empower women in the love of Jesus Christ and the truth of God's Word. Through our online Bible Studies, Daily Devotional and mobile app women all over the world are finding freedom, wholeness, and satisfaction in Jesus Christ. From the woman on her morning commute to the new mother nursing her infant at night, or the student on her way home from class; Beloved Women's free online resources are helping women worldwide connect with God daily in powerful, relevant, and simple ways. In a world full of artificial happiness and temporary satisfaction Beloved Women is dedicated to empower women with the authentic love of Jesus Christ and the lasting truth of God's Word.

you are loved

31077438R00078

Made in the USA
San Bernardino, CA
02 April 2019